No Heat on the Second Floor
How to fire your plumb̶̶̶̶̶̶̶̶

A comprehensive step by step guide for D   ...no
own houses from Victorian age to new construction, with malfunctioning boilers that are considering installing a new system because the old
one doesn't fully heat the whole house. It includes instructions on diagnosing your systems problem, isolating blockages, how to fix the ever
popular no heat on the second floor problem in a hot water circulation
system. It includes instructions on changing corroded automatic feeder
valve, changing corroded shutoff valves, maintaining the circulation
pump, bleeding the system, maintaining an old hot water boiler, soldering copper pipes, working with black pipes and more. A must have for
DIYers and homeowners who are contemplating a twenty five to thirty
thousand dollar fix of replacing their entire hot water circulatory system
on advice from their plumber versus a less than one thousand dollar solution to cold radiator pipes. Written for DIYers and homeowners interested in demystifying why their radiators above the second floor are
cold, and to gain an overall understanding of how their hot water heating system functions.

Contents

No Heat on the Second Floor
How To Fire Your Plumber

First of all, I'm not a Plumber, I'm not licensed, nor do I play one on TV, but after years of getting hosed by plumbers, I finally built up the nerve to fire my plumber. I figured the way my plumber fixes stuff around the house, you couldn't do worse fixing it yourself. My journey started when I purchased a 100+ year old Victorian that had the original boiler still installed and working. It had just one problem, little or no heat on the second and third floor radiators, problems that some of you with brand new houses are facing today. I called my plumber up and he said I should replace it. My response was what's wrong with it? It was old. What else was wrong? Nothing. Can you fix it? He said no problem. I'm not going to toss it just because its' old, so I had him fix it. He proceeded to bleed my boiler [drain the boiler of rusty water to make the boiler run more efficient]. The bleeding proved to be a temporary fix because no sooner than he hit the door after collecting his fee, or at worse the next week, I'd have sporadic heat on the second and third floor radiators.

The bleeding didn't work, and I'd spend the next three months chasing him to come back and fix it for, you guessed it another fee. I tried bleeding the radiator valves myself, but nothing ever happened. According to all the plumbing books, the radiator valve would release the air in the system until water came out of the valve, then close the valve. But for the life of me the air would start hissing, and then just die. I didn't even have to close the valve. The hissing of bleeding the radiator would just stop and for years I left the valves open because the water never traveled up to the second floor radiators let alone the third floor ones. To make a long story short, his bleeding of my pockets lasted for seven years until finally I got sick of being cold, sick of hearing my wife and kids complain about being cold, sick of reading plumbing books written by professional plumbers that went on and on with plumbing jargon that only make sense to plumbers with no pictures of what they were describing and didn't just tell you how to fix your problem. Sick of buying plumbing books with only a page or two dedicated to heat with useless information. Sick of chasing my plumber for an appointment which he would break every time, and then when he showed up I'd pay him for the same results. One very cold weekend, I decided to fix it myself, figuring I couldn't do any worse than my plumber.

My biggest fear was I would cause a flood. After reading enough plumbing books without getting a clear idea of how to fix my problem and filling in the blanks by traveling to Lowe's or Home Depot and asking questions about the 'thingy' that connects to the other 'thingy' and getting that dumb stare from the plumbers because I didn't know the name of the part I was trying to describe, and hearing you have to 'bleed' the radiator ten thousand times, It finally hit me...

A combination of bleeding the radiators and draining the boiler of the water left the system dry until no water was left in the system. The system was out of water, after tracing the water back to the main, I realized that the pipe was cold before the Automatic Feeder Valve and after it. I had found the problem. The automatic feeder valve was corroded or clogged and no water was passing through it. It had to be replaced; the system was after all over 70 years old. After determining the problem, I called other plumber services, but was told that they would charge a $300 diagnostic fee. One problem, I already found the problem, they were going to charge me to find the problem that I had already found. In addition,, they wouldn't use the parts I had purchased and they'd only guarantee parts they sell and would bill me a huge markup and since the weekend was considered emergency plumbing hours, it was double the hourly fee. And since I wasn't a plumber, my assessment of the problem wasn't valid. In other words, since you're paying by the hour, get out your checkbook. After staring at the boiler for hours, I overcame my fear that I would flood my house and decided to fix it myself. Here's what I did.

Your boiler, do you need to replace it?

The first step to firing your plumber is to realize that contrary to your plumbers recommendation, you don't need a new boiler, new copper pipes, or a new system because that will not only be super expensive, but except in extreme cases of vandalism where vandals steal your boiler and rip out your copper pipes, it's also unnecessary; a new system will run you $25,000 - $30,000 installed and a new boiler $5- $10k (not including installation) is built to last 3-5 years before it breaks down and your plumber will recommend that you buy another new unit when it does. Why do that when in most cases for under $1,000 you could fix and maintain your current boiler. Understand that all your boiler does is heat the water. Let me repeat for emphasis,

all your boiler does is heat the water.

That's it! gas or oil, the boilers job is simply to heat the water in the system, so unless your boiler doesn't heat the water, it should be fixed not discarded.

Your old boiler, if it's broke, fix it.

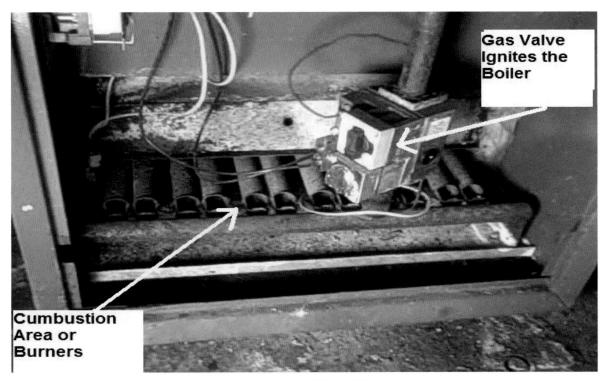

Gas Valve Ignites the Boiler

Cumbustion Area or Burners

Inside view of an old boiler.

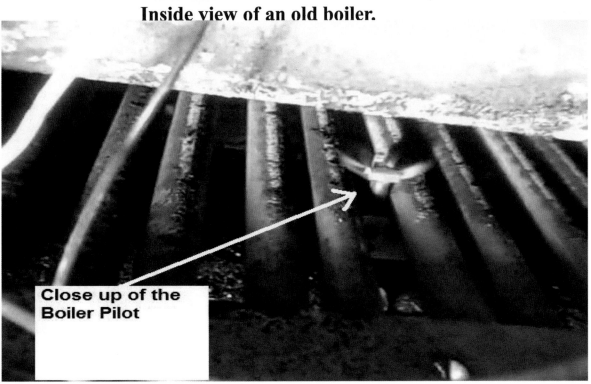

Close up of the Boiler Pilot

Boiler Maintenance

All boilers have a furnace, a pilot, and an ignition. The furnace needs to be cleaned (vacuumed) periodically, once a year. The pilot keeps the flame from the gas line lit. The gas valve provides the ignition to light the furnace every time the thermostat calls for heat (thermostat temperature is above the current temperature in the house). If the thermostat calls for heat (you'll hear a clicking sound like when you turn on your gas stove), but never comes on, either the gas valve needs to be replaced ($150 Honeywell) or the contact unit needs to be scraped due to corrosion. You can call in a boiler specialist, not a plumber to fix it for about $75-$100.

The Circulation Pump

The circulator pump in your system is the workhorse. Its' job is to transport the water from the basement to the top floor in your house or building. Get this, the same pump that supplies your second or third floor with hot water is in all likelihood a Bell & Gossett Pump (B&G), and is the same heavy duty pump most commercial buildings rely on to circulate hot water from the basement to the top floor using gravity. These things are mechanical and over time will experience wear and tear and eventually will require maintenance to keep functioning just like a car. If all you do is put gas in your car, sooner or later you're going to have to oil and replace worn parts. If you don't, your car or boiler won't perform its' function and you'll have problems. If your boiler stops working, here are the symptoms and the remedies.

Fixing a leaking Circulator Pump

The pump will leak overtime due to a worn paper gasket that connects the pump to the system. The pumps interior parts will need to be oiled and eventually replaced due to wear and tear unless you have a self contained unit without ball bearings. The paper gasket should be replaced with a more durable rubber gasket.

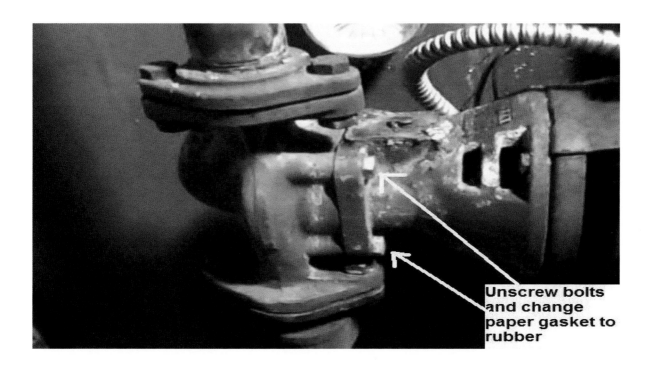

Unscrew bolts and change paper gasket to rubber

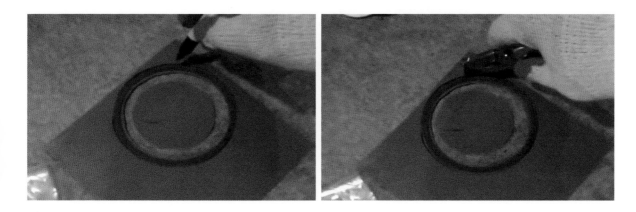

Measure the gasket and replace the gasket with a more durable rubber gasket that withstands the extreme heat a lot better than paper and won't wear out as fast over time. The gasket is the equivalent of a washer on a pipe, once the new washer is installed, no more leaks. Purchase the identical size paper gasket, and a sheet of rubber at your local plumbing supply store. Trace the gasket onto the rubber, cut out the rubber gasket. Unscrew the pump bolts, install the new gasket, and re-install bolts on the pump.

Or Just buy a new pump

You could also choose to replace the pump with a new self contained unit that doesn't need to be oiled or maintained. These units cost $350 at your local plumbing supply store and will save you the time to deconstruct the pump to replace worn parts. A complete guide to repairing your pump can be found on http://www.bellgossett.com/homeowners/HT-pumps.asp

Your Circulatory System

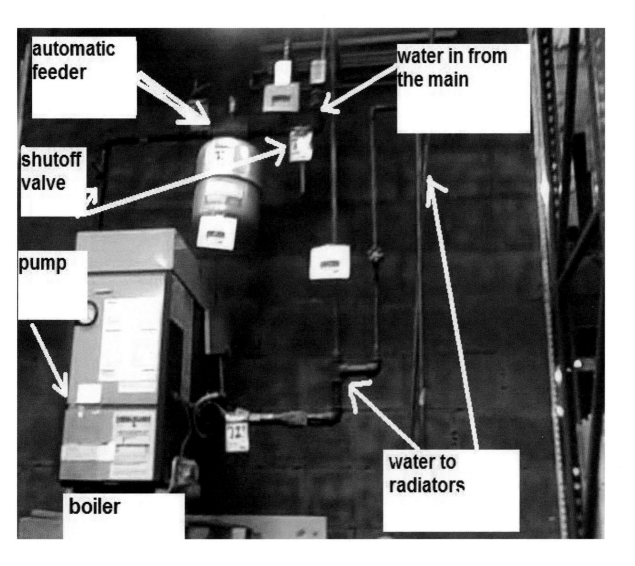

Understanding the anatomy of your circulatory system is the key to maintaining and fixing your system. Any hot water system relies on water from the main water supply from the street with two shutoff valves in front of and behind the automatic feeder valve. The automatic feeder valve does exactly what its name says; it automatically feeds the system the water to be heated up by the boiler for transport throughout the system via the pump.

No Heat in one or more radiator

For those of you suffering through no heat on the second floor and up, understand that you have a blockage due to corrosion in one or more of your pipes that has to be detected and removed in order for the water to get to the radiators on the top floor.

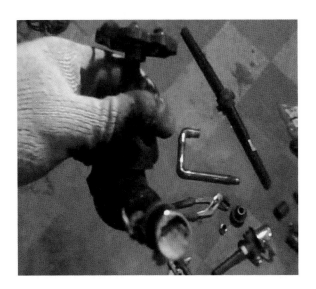 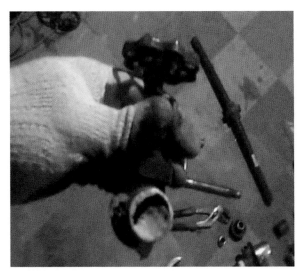

Your first course of action before you start replacing pipes should be to find out where the blockage is in your system by 'bleeding' (drain) the water in the system. Bleeding the pipes releases the sediment trapped in the system, if the system isn't bled (flushed), the pipes corrode from the inside and clogs the system over time.

Diagnosing the problem
by bleeding the system

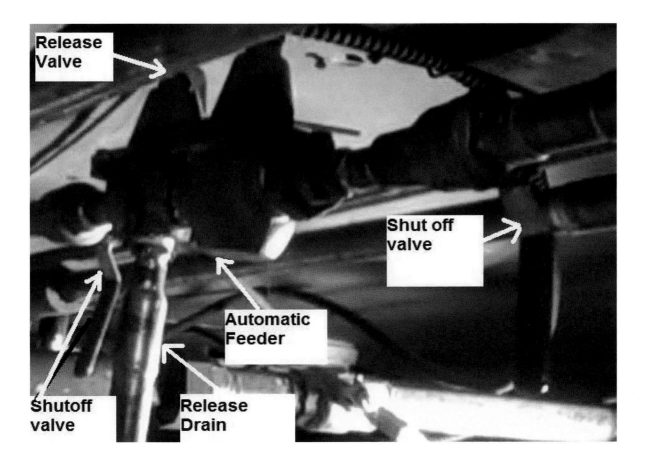

1) Locate the Automatic Feeder valve.
2) Trace the pipe from the main water supply into the boiler, the automatic feeder will be the on the line before the pipe goes into the boiler. The automatic feed has a shutoff valve immediately before and immediately after it, and an emergency release valve located at the bottom of the valve.

3) Close the shutoff valve before the automatic feed valve. Attached to the bottom of the automatic feeder valve is an emergency release valve with a shutoff valve on the end to release water from the system.

Bleeding the system

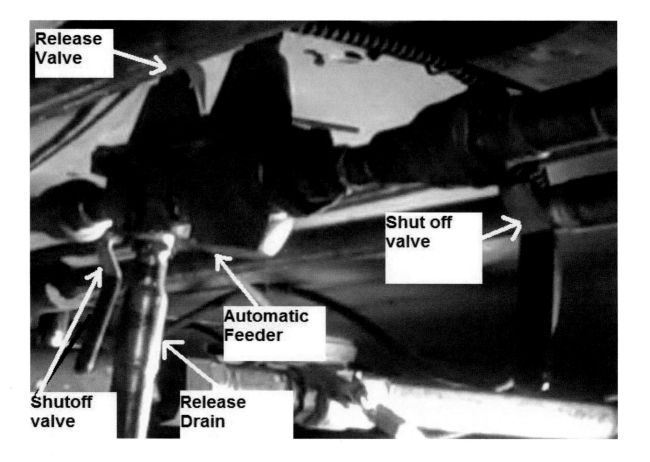

1) Get a bucket or two to catch the water.
2) Close the shutoff valve **before** the automatic feeder valve, closer to the main.
3) Open the shutoff valve at the end of the emergency release drain.
4) Open shutoff valve **after** the automatic feeder, closer to the boiler.
5) Release the water in the pipes by lifting the release valve on top of the automatic feeder. Make sure you close the shutoff valve before the feeder, if you don't you'll be emptying water directly from the main water supply and you don't have enough buckets to drain the city's water supply. If you've drained 6 five gallon buckets and the water is still flowing heavy, then your shutoff valve before the automatic feeder is probably still open.
6) Drain the water until its empty.

Bleeding the boiler

Boiler drain

1) Locate the boiler drain valve on the boiler and repeat the bleeding process by opening the valves and drain until empty into your bucket.
2) Now that the system is empty, close the release valves on the top of the automatic feeder.
3) Open the shutoff valve before the automatic feeder to fill the system with water. Most systems are made of metal that corrodes in water. Bleeding the pipes releases the sediment trapped in the system, but because the feeder is relatively small, it corrodes and gets clogged over time.

Engage the boiler

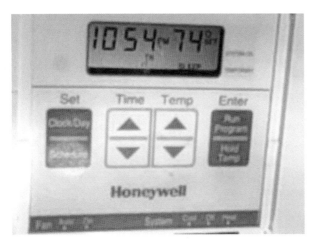 

Engage the boiler to test the system by setting the thermostat to a temperature higher than the homes current temperature, eg. if the current temperature is 74 degrees, set the thermostat on 78 degrees by pressing hold to override the current setting, then increasing the temperature to 78. The boiler will only engage if the thermostat is set to a temperature above the current temperature. To deactivate the boiler at the end of your system check, press run program.

Bleeding the radiators

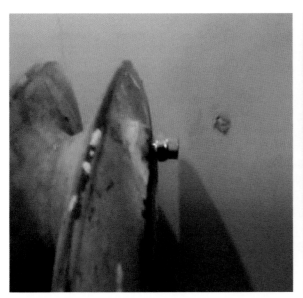

1) Open the release valve located on the side of all the radiators using a 'plumbers tool' ($1) shown above (r) to release the air pockets trapped in the system.
2) Only open one at a time.
3) You should hear the hissing of air being released. If the hissing dies and no water comes out of the valve, you likely have a blockage due to corrosion probably in your automatic feeder valve or a shutoff valve feeding that line somewhere in your system.
4) Repeat the step to all of the radiators on the cold floors. If water comes out of the valve and the radiator doesn't get hot, the cold radiator line might be corroded and not the system indicating that a shutoff valve or union on the cold line is corroded and not the automatic feeder. If all the radiators have no hot water being released from the open valves after the hissing stops, the blockage is something that affects the entire system which would likely be the automatic feeder valve.

Isolating the blockage

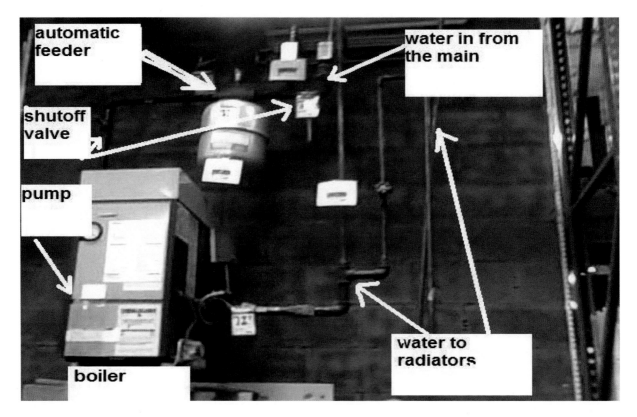

1) Does the automatic feeder need replacing ($100), or one or more shut-off valves ($15)?
2) If all the radiators on the cold floors are bled and no water comes out of the valves, you have a system wide problem.
3) The automatic feeder is located before the boiler and therefore affects all the radiators in the house. The boiler then feeds the individual radiator lines all of which will have a shutoff valve. If the cold radiators are random, then the blockage could be a local shutoff valve or union. The individual shutoff valves affect only the line it feeds.
4) Feel the pipe after the automatic feeder. If it's hot, the feeder is working properly, if its cold the feeder needs to be replaced.
5) Why is the first floor radiators hot or warm and not the upper floors, because even if there's no water in the system, the boiler being on will build up steam which will heat the nearest radiators on the first floor like in a steam system. It won't be enough to travel up to the upper floors.

Replacing the Automatic Feeder
Using black pipe

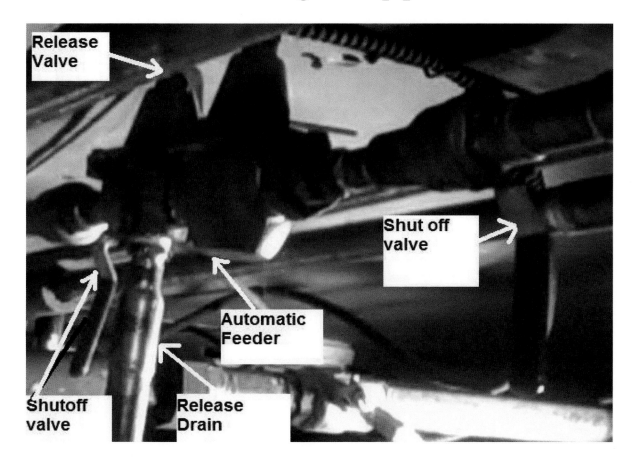

Release Valve

Shut off valve

Automatic Feeder

Shutoff valve

Release Drain

Tools needed

Jig saw

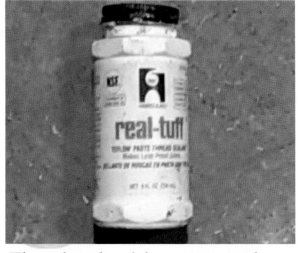

Thread sealant/pipe compound

Teflon tape

Two nipples

Two wrenches

Pipe union

New automatic feeder

Tape measure

Replacing the automatic feeder

Step 1

1) Measure the length of the black pipe after the automatic feeder valve and purchase two nipples that equal the total measurement of the pipe you're about to replace from a plumbing supply store or your local Home Depot.

2) You will need to know the radius (it will most likely be 3/4 inch or 1/2 inch). You can mix and match the pipes they come in sizes starting at ½ inch length 'nipples' all the way up to 10' lengths if your required length is not available. You will also need to purchase a union to for the final connection of the two new pipes.

3) Shut off the water from the shutoff valve **before** the automatic feeder valve.

4) Drain the system of the water via the emergency water release located on the bottom of the automatic feeder valve.

Cut the pipe

Step 2

1) Use jig saw or a grinder with a metal blade to cut the black pipe immediately **after** the feeder.
2) Tip: Jigsaw blades get hot fast and break, so have a bucket of water near to cool off the blade periodically.
3) Remove cut pipes using two wrench. One to hold the pipe still and one to loosen.
4) Remove the automatic feeder emergency release valve located on the bottom of the feeder.
5) Use the wrenches to remove the automatic feeder from the uncut pipe. Why not cut the pipe before the feeder? Because you will need the threaded end to reconnect the new feeder.
6) Tip: If the pipe joint is stuck, try heating the fitting with a torch to loosen the joint.

Step 3

1) Wrap the male threading on the replacement nipples 12-14 times with teflon tape then cover the wrap with thread sealant (pipe compound) to guard against leaks.

2) Normally, plumbers use either teflon or thread sealant, but if the system leaks, you'll have to shut off the water, undo the leaking joint, reseal the joint, then put it back together. I err on the side of caution by using both.

Step 4

1) Wipe automatic feeder with pipe compound on both female threaded ends.
2) Attach the new automatic feeder valve to the threaded uncut pipe you removed the faulty automatic feeder from with two wrenches, use one wrench to hold the pipe steady and tighten with the other wrench until the feeder valve is upright.

Step 5

1) Use two nipples totaling the measurement of the cut pipe to replace the cut pipe. The first nipple will connect to the feeder, the second will replace the cut pipe you just removed from its threaded connection. Both nipples will then be connected with a union, connecting the union is the last step.

2) Attach one nipple to automatic feeder using two wrenches. Hold the feeder steady while turning the nipple clockwise until tight.

3) Attach the other nipple to replace the cut pipe you removed. Tighten with two wrenches.

Step 6
1) Cover inside of both female ends of union with thread sealant.
2) Attach union to both remaining ends of pipes and tighten each end.
3) Do not overtighten the union as it will break.
4) Turn on water slowly and check for leaks.

Replacing the Automatic Feeder
using copper pipe

If your pipes are copper, you're going to have to learn how to 'sweat' or soldier the pipes and fittings together. You can choose to use all copper or you can go from black to copper using threaded copper fittings as a converter from black to copper. The reason some people use copper over black pipe is copper is more flexible, it is also more expensive than relatively cheap black pipe.

Screw feeder to uncut threaded pipe

Attach release valve last

Soldier to cut pipe

Tools needed

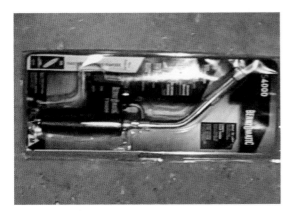

You'll need a Torch (Bernzomatic T4000 for professionals or better) if you buy the cheap ones, after about a month of heavy use, you'll be buying it

You'll need propane tanks $3 always buy 3, believe me, you'll always run out of propane when the plumbing supply store is closed.

Copper fittings that are the identical size (1/2". 3/4", or 1") and shape of the fitting you're about to replace. Male threaded fitting, reducing coupler, elbow, and a coupler.

A tub of solder paste   A roll of soldier

A roll of abrasive cloth 20 grit size

You'll need copper pipe. Buy two 10 foot pipes in the size to replace the pipe.

You'll need two heavy duty wrench to hold the fittings while you sweat them.   Also to remove threaded fittings by holding the pipe steady while turning the fitting in counter clockwise.

You'll need a pipe cutter ($179) to cut the pipe   to the exact size you need.

 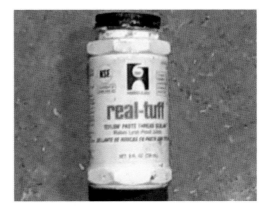

Teflon tape.   Pipe sealant

Replacing the Automatic Feeder
using copper

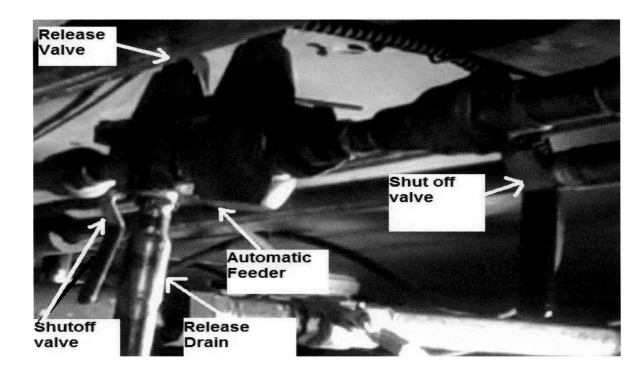

Step 1
1) Turn off the water from the shutoff valve **before** the automatic feeder, if you're not sure which is which, just shut off the water from the main.
2) Open the shutoff valve after the automatic feeder.
3) Drain the system by opening the release valve on top of the automatic feeder.
4) Set a bucket to catch the water. It should fill up five to six buckets.

Step 2
1) Measure the pipe you're replacing.

Step 3
1) Cut the pipe before the automatic feeder (**after** the shutoff
valve, furthest from the boiler)

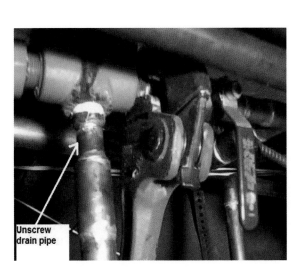

Unscrew
drain pipe

Step 4
1) Unscrew the feeder drain pipe located at the bot-
    tom of the automatic feeder.
2) Remove the automatic feeder valve by holding
    the pipe steady with one wrench and removing
    the feeder with the other wrench.

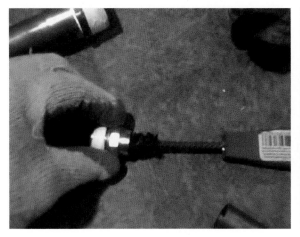 

Step 6
1) Score two male threaded 1/2 inch fittings (most automatic feeders use 1/2 inch threaded fittings).

Step 7
1) Measure the pipes you are replacing and cut to size.

Step 8

1) Cut the new pipe to size.

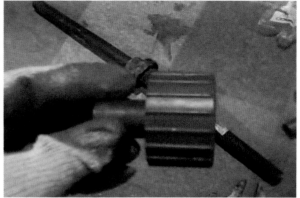

Step 9

1) Score the outside of both ends of the replacement pipes so that the soldier can attach to the pipe.

Step 10

1) Wipe all ends of the pipe with soldier paste.

Step 11

1) Dry fit fitting to replacement pipe to male fitting.

Step 12
1) Wipe both threaded female
ends of the new automatic feeder
with pipe sealant.

Step 13
1) Wrap male threaded fitting
with teflon tape then pipe sealant.

Step 14
1) Screw male fitting to feeder
tighten with a wrench.

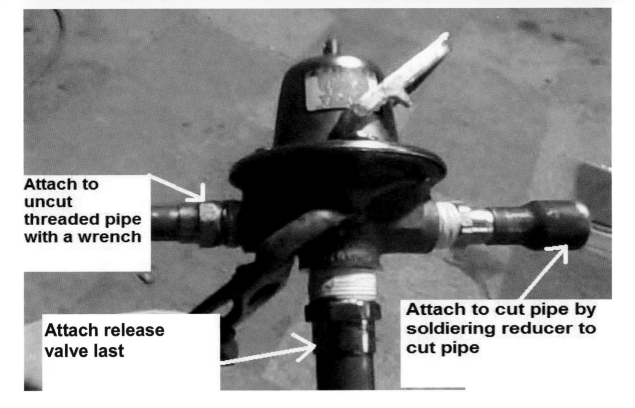

Attach to uncut threaded pipe with a wrench

Attach release valve last

Attach to cut pipe by soldiering reducer to cut pipe

Reassemble the automatic feeder onto the system by attaching the feeder to the uncut threaded pipe.

Attach the new pipe to cut the pipe with a coupler or a reducer coupler (one end is 1/2 inch the other is 3/4 or 1 inch) if the cut pipe is bigger than the feeder which usually comes in 1/2 inch standard.

Sometimes the cut pipe won't dry fit into the coupler, use the abrasive cloth or a grinder to smooth the edge of the pipe to fit the coupler.

Soldering the copper joints

Screw feeder to uncut threaded pipe

Attach release valve last

Soldier to cut pipe

12) Connect the pipes by soldiering the pipes. Apply heat using the torch to the heat fittings only, not the pipe.
13) Test if pipe is hot enough by touching the joint with the soldier. If the soldier melts, use enough soldier to hold fitting together, stop when the melted soldier flows over the top of the fitting, wipe away the excess soldier with a damp cloth. Joint hardens in 30 seconds.
14) Soldier all joints with fittings, **not** the threaded joints.
15) Wait 15 minutes for pipes to cool before slowly turning on the water to check for leaks.

Undoing a sweated joint

If you need to undo a soldiered joint;

Heat the fitting until the soldier melts.

Using two pliers, pull the joints apart.

Clean the soldier from the fitting and the pipe using a damp cloth and scoring the fitting. You will have to repeat the step several times to remove the soldier from the fitting or pipe or you could just purchase a new fitting.

Replacing a corroded shutoff valve

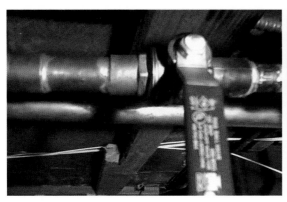

If replacing the automatic feeder doesn't result in hot water traveling up to the all the radiators, you might have a corroded shutoff valve(s) leading up to the cold radiator(s) that needs to be replaced.

To troubleshoot, locate the line leading to the cold radiator from the basement.

Feel the pipe to see if the pipe is hot leading up to the line of the cold radiator. If you've got the right line, you'll find the spot where the pipe goes from hot to cold by feeling the pipe along the line. At that point on the pipe, one side will be piping hot and after a shutoff valve, union or some other connection device it will be cold.

Tools needed for black pipe

Jig saw

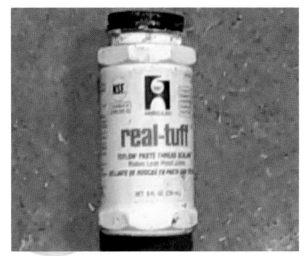

Thread sealant/pipe compound

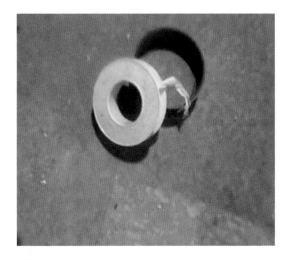

Teflon tape

One inch nipple

Two wrenches

Pipe union

Tape measure

Threaded shutoff valve

Replacing the shutoff valve using black pipe

1) Shutting off the water at the automatic feeder.

2) Drain the system of water into a bucket.

3) Cut the faulty shutoff valve in two, and remove it the pieces from the line. Be careful not to cut the threaded pipe that's attached to it or you'll be replacing that pipe too.

4) Wrap the two male threaded ends of the remaining pipe with teflon tape.

5) Wipe the female ends of the new shutoff valve with pipe compound.

Replacing shutoff pipe using black pipe

1) Connect the new shutoff valve using two wrench, to one end of the male threaded pipe.

2) Wrap a 1 inch nipple with teflon tape and wipe with pipe compound.

3) Wipe both female ends of the union with pipe compound.

4) Connect a 1 inch nipple, to the shutoff valve.

5) Connect the nipple to the remaining pipe using the union and tighten, don't overtighten union.

Tools needed for copper pipe

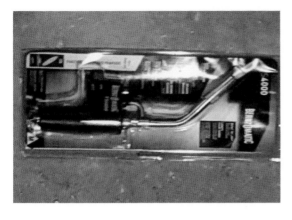

You'll need a Torch (Bernzomatic T4000 for professionals or better) if you buy the cheap ones, after about a month of heavy use, you'll be buying it

You'll need propane tanks $3 always buy 3, believe me, you'll always run out of propane when the plumbing supply store is closed.

Pipe cutter

Copper coupler identical size of pipe (1/2". 3/4", or 1")

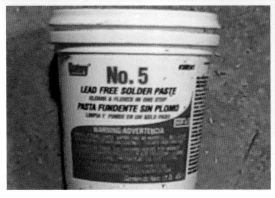

A tub of solder paste

A roll of soldier

A roll of abrasive cloth 20 grit size

Copper pipe

Sweat shutoff valve

Replacing the shutoff valve using copper

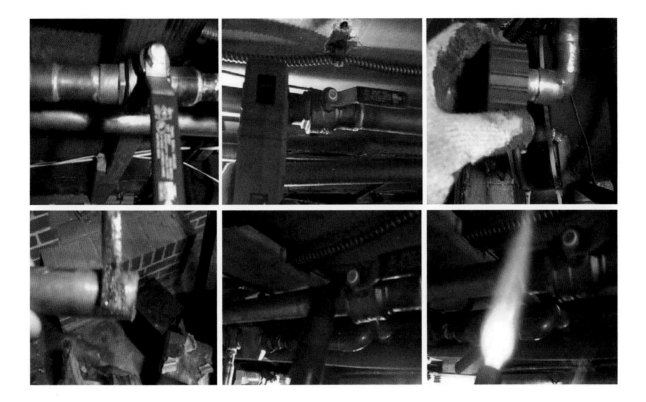

1) Shutting off the water at the automatic feeder.
2) Drain the system of water into a bucket.
3) Cut copper pipe on both sides of the faulty shutoff valve and remove valve.
4) Score both ends of the cut pipes.
5) Apply soldier paste to both scored ends of the pipes.
6) Score the female ends of the sweated shutoff valve.
7) Apply soldier paste to female ends of scored shutoff valve.
8) Attached sweated shutoff valve to one end of cut pipe.

Replacing the shutoff valve using copper

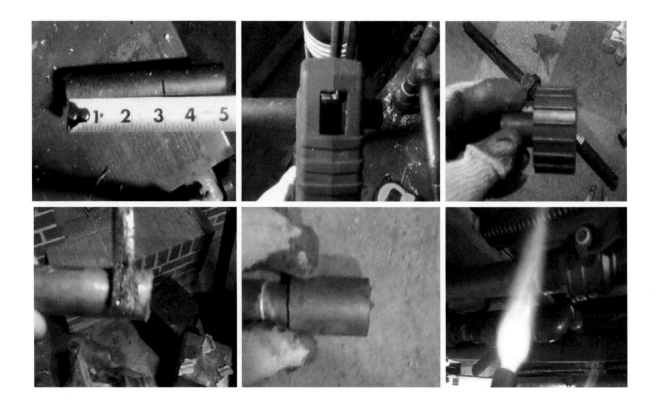

1) Measure distance from remaining cutoff valve to inside of the shutoff valve.
2) Cut new copper pipe to fit missing piece.
3) Score both ends of replacement pipe.
4) Apply soldier paste to both ends of replacement pipe.
5) Attach new pipe to shutoff valve and cut pipe using a coupler.
6) Soldier all new fittings with torch.
7) Wipe soldiered ends with a damp cloth before soldier dries.
8) Wait fifteen minutes before turning on water.

Some of the shutoff valves are sold as sweat or threaded. Purchase the identical fitting you are replacing, but you aren't limited to that. Sometimes you might visualize an easier way of accomplishing the same or a better result. Just be prepared to visualize the end product if you deviate from the fitting or pipe you are replacing and use dry fitting to get a visual before you soldier.

Dedication

This book is dedicated to my wife Nik, who inspired me to put into words the instructions floating around in my head. This book is for everyone who asked how did I fix my heat because they were having the same problems with their hot water circulatory system and didn't know how to fix it. Hopefully, after reading this book, you'll have a background knowledge on how your hot water circulatory system works and how to fix any problems that pop up. With the help of this book, you'll never have to call your plumber again.

Look for our upcoming website
www.noheatonthesecondfloor.com

No Heat on the second floor,
How to fire your plumber

A comprehensive step by step guide for DIYers and homeowners who own houses from Victorian age to new construction, with malfunctioning boilers that are considering installing a new system because the old one doesn't fully heat the whole house. It includes instructions on diagnosing your systems problem, isolating blockages, how to fix the ever popular no heat on the second floor problem in a hot water circulation system. It includes instructions on changing corroded automatic feeder valve, changing corroded shutoff valves, maintaining the circulation pump, bleeding the system, maintaining an old hot water boiler, soldering copper pipes, working with black pipes and more. A must have for DIYers and homeowners who are contemplating a twenty five to thirty thousand dollar fix of replacing their entire hot water circulatory system on advice from their plumber versus a less than one thousand dollar solution to cold radiator pipes. Written for DIYers and homeowners interested in demystifying why their radiators above the second floor are cold, and to gain an overall understanding of how their hot water heating system functions.

Printed in Great Britain
by Amazon